50 Chili and Stew Recipes for Home

By: Kelly Johnson

Table of Contents

- Classic Beef Chili
- White Chicken Chili
- Vegetarian Black Bean Chili
- Spicy Turkey Chili
- Smoky Chipotle Chili
- Cincinnati Chili
- Beef and Bean Chili
- Sweet Potato and Lentil Stew
- Hearty Vegetable Stew
- Chicken and Dumpling Stew
- Southwest Beef Stew
- Pork Green Chili
- Moroccan Chickpea Stew
- Creamy Potato and Leek Stew
- Spicy Sausage and Kale Stew
- Buffalo Chicken Chili
- Coconut Curry Lentil Stew
- Tomato and Basil Stew
- Ratatouille Stew
- Coconut Lime Chicken Stew
- Classic Beef Stew
- Italian Sausage and Peppers Chili
- Chili con Carne
- Jambalaya Stew
- Smoky BBQ Bean Stew
- Turkey and Sweet Potato Chili
- Mediterranean Vegetable Stew
- Mushroom and Barley Stew
- Beer-Braised Beef Stew
- Indian-Spiced Lentil Chili
- Curried Butternut Squash Stew
- Chicken and Rice Stew
- Chili Verde
- Eggplant and Chickpea Stew
- Beef and Ale Stew
- Moroccan Lamb Stew
- Rustic Potato and Bacon Stew
- Spicy Thai Coconut Chili
- Cajun Chicken and Sausage Stew

- Beef and Vegetable Chili
- Thai Green Curry Stew
- Rustic Italian Bean Stew
- Sweet Corn and Chicken Chili
- Lamb and White Bean Stew
- Thai Red Curry Beef Stew
- Classic Split Pea Soup
- Black Eyed Pea and Collard Green Stew
- Tomato Basil Chickpea Stew
- Spicy Pumpkin and Black Bean Chili
- Fish and Vegetable Stew

Classic Beef Chili

Ingredients:

- 1 lb ground beef
- 1 onion, chopped
- 2 cloves garlic, minced
- 1 can (15 oz) kidney beans, rinsed and drained
- 1 can (15 oz) diced tomatoes
- 2 tablespoons chili powder
- 1 teaspoon cumin
- Salt and pepper to taste

Instructions:

1. In a large pot, brown the ground beef over medium heat. Drain excess fat.
2. Add onion and garlic, and sauté until softened.
3. Stir in kidney beans, diced tomatoes, chili powder, cumin, salt, and pepper.
4. Simmer for 20-30 minutes, stirring occasionally. Serve hot.

White Chicken Chili

Ingredients:

- 1 lb cooked chicken, shredded
- 1 can (15 oz) white beans, rinsed and drained
- 1 can (15 oz) diced green chilies
- 1 onion, chopped
- 2 cloves garlic, minced
- 4 cups chicken broth
- 1 teaspoon cumin
- 1 teaspoon oregano
- Salt and pepper to taste

Instructions:

1. In a pot, sauté onion and garlic until softened.
2. Add shredded chicken, white beans, green chilies, chicken broth, cumin, oregano, salt, and pepper.
3. Bring to a boil, then reduce heat and simmer for 20 minutes. Serve warm.

Vegetarian Black Bean Chili

Ingredients:

- 2 cans (15 oz) black beans, rinsed and drained
- 1 can (15 oz) diced tomatoes
- 1 onion, chopped
- 1 bell pepper, diced
- 2 cloves garlic, minced
- 2 tablespoons chili powder
- 1 teaspoon cumin
- Salt and pepper to taste

Instructions:

1. In a large pot, sauté onion, bell pepper, and garlic until softened.
2. Add black beans, diced tomatoes, chili powder, cumin, salt, and pepper.
3. Simmer for 20-30 minutes, stirring occasionally. Serve hot.

Spicy Turkey Chili

Ingredients:

- 1 lb ground turkey
- 1 onion, chopped
- 2 cloves garlic, minced
- 1 can (15 oz) diced tomatoes
- 1 can (15 oz) kidney beans, rinsed and drained
- 1 tablespoon chili powder
- 1 teaspoon cayenne pepper
- Salt and pepper to taste

Instructions:

1. In a large pot, brown the ground turkey over medium heat.
2. Add onion and garlic, and sauté until softened.
3. Stir in diced tomatoes, kidney beans, chili powder, cayenne pepper, salt, and pepper.
4. Simmer for 20-30 minutes. Serve hot.

Smoky Chipotle Chili

Ingredients:

- 1 lb ground beef or turkey
- 1 onion, chopped
- 2 cloves garlic, minced
- 1 can (15 oz) black beans, rinsed and drained
- 1 can (15 oz) diced tomatoes
- 2-3 chipotle peppers in adobo sauce, chopped
- 1 teaspoon cumin
- Salt and pepper to taste

Instructions:

1. In a large pot, brown the ground meat over medium heat.
2. Add onion and garlic, and sauté until softened.
3. Stir in black beans, diced tomatoes, chipotle peppers, cumin, salt, and pepper.
4. Simmer for 20-30 minutes. Serve hot.

Cincinnati Chili

Ingredients:

- 1 lb ground beef
- 1 onion, chopped
- 2 cloves garlic, minced
- 1 can (15 oz) tomato sauce
- 1 tablespoon chili powder
- 1 teaspoon cinnamon
- 1 teaspoon cumin
- 1/2 cup water
- Salt and pepper to taste
- Serve with spaghetti and cheese (optional)

Instructions:

1. In a pot, brown the ground beef, then drain excess fat.
2. Add onion and garlic, and sauté until softened.
3. Stir in tomato sauce, chili powder, cinnamon, cumin, water, salt, and pepper.
4. Simmer for 30-40 minutes. Serve over spaghetti with cheese if desired.

Beef and Bean Chili

Ingredients:

- 1 lb ground beef
- 1 can (15 oz) kidney beans, rinsed and drained
- 1 can (15 oz) black beans, rinsed and drained
- 1 can (15 oz) diced tomatoes
- 1 onion, chopped
- 2 cloves garlic, minced
- 2 tablespoons chili powder
- Salt and pepper to taste

Instructions:

1. In a large pot, brown the ground beef and drain excess fat.
2. Add onion and garlic, and sauté until softened.
3. Stir in kidney beans, black beans, diced tomatoes, chili powder, salt, and pepper.
4. Simmer for 20-30 minutes. Serve hot.

Sweet Potato and Lentil Stew

Ingredients:

- 2 cups sweet potatoes, diced
- 1 cup lentils, rinsed
- 1 onion, chopped
- 2 carrots, diced
- 2 cloves garlic, minced
- 4 cups vegetable broth
- 1 teaspoon cumin
- Salt and pepper to taste

Instructions:

1. In a pot, sauté onion, carrots, and garlic until softened.
2. Add sweet potatoes, lentils, vegetable broth, cumin, salt, and pepper.
3. Bring to a boil, then reduce heat and simmer for 30-40 minutes until lentils and sweet potatoes are tender. Serve warm.

Enjoy your hearty chili and stew recipes!

Hearty Vegetable Stew

Ingredients:

- 2 tablespoons olive oil
- 1 onion, chopped
- 2 carrots, diced
- 2 celery stalks, diced
- 3 cloves garlic, minced
- 4 cups vegetable broth
- 1 can (15 oz) diced tomatoes
- 2 cups potatoes, cubed
- 1 zucchini, diced
- 1 cup green beans, trimmed and cut
- 1 teaspoon thyme
- Salt and pepper to taste

Instructions:

1. In a large pot, heat olive oil over medium heat.
2. Add onion, carrots, celery, and garlic, and sauté until softened.
3. Stir in vegetable broth, diced tomatoes, potatoes, zucchini, green beans, thyme, salt, and pepper.
4. Bring to a boil, then reduce heat and simmer for 30 minutes. Serve warm.

Chicken and Dumpling Stew

Ingredients:

- 1 lb chicken breast, diced
- 2 tablespoons olive oil
- 1 onion, chopped
- 2 carrots, diced
- 2 celery stalks, diced
- 4 cups chicken broth
- 1 cup frozen peas
- 1 teaspoon thyme
- Salt and pepper to taste
- 1 package refrigerated biscuit dough

Instructions:

1. In a large pot, heat olive oil over medium heat.
2. Add onion, carrots, and celery, and sauté until softened.
3. Add chicken and cook until no longer pink.
4. Stir in chicken broth, peas, thyme, salt, and pepper.
5. Bring to a boil, then reduce heat.
6. Drop pieces of biscuit dough on top, cover, and simmer for 15-20 minutes until dumplings are cooked. Serve warm.

Southwest Beef Stew

Ingredients:

- 1 lb beef stew meat, cut into cubes
- 2 tablespoons olive oil
- 1 onion, chopped
- 2 cloves garlic, minced
- 2 carrots, diced
- 1 bell pepper, diced
- 1 can (15 oz) diced tomatoes
- 2 cups beef broth
- 1 can (15 oz) black beans, rinsed and drained
- 2 tablespoons chili powder
- Salt and pepper to taste

Instructions:

1. In a large pot, heat olive oil over medium-high heat.
2. Add beef and brown on all sides.
3. Add onion, garlic, carrots, and bell pepper, and sauté until softened.
4. Stir in diced tomatoes, beef broth, black beans, chili powder, salt, and pepper.
5. Bring to a boil, then reduce heat and simmer for 1.5 to 2 hours. Serve warm.

Pork Green Chili

Ingredients:

- 1 lb pork shoulder, diced
- 2 tablespoons olive oil
- 1 onion, chopped
- 2 cloves garlic, minced
- 2-3 green chilies, diced
- 1 can (15 oz) diced tomatoes
- 2 cups chicken broth
- 1 teaspoon cumin
- Salt and pepper to taste

Instructions:

1. In a large pot, heat olive oil over medium-high heat.
2. Add pork and brown on all sides.
3. Add onion and garlic, and sauté until softened.
4. Stir in green chilies, diced tomatoes, chicken broth, cumin, salt, and pepper.
5. Bring to a boil, then reduce heat and simmer for 1.5 to 2 hours. Serve warm.

Moroccan Chickpea Stew

Ingredients:

- 2 tablespoons olive oil
- 1 onion, chopped
- 2 cloves garlic, minced
- 1 can (15 oz) chickpeas, rinsed and drained
- 1 can (15 oz) diced tomatoes
- 2 cups vegetable broth
- 2 carrots, diced
- 1 zucchini, diced
- 1 tablespoon Moroccan spice blend (or cumin, coriander, cinnamon)
- Salt and pepper to taste

Instructions:

1. In a large pot, heat olive oil over medium heat.
2. Add onion and garlic, and sauté until softened.
3. Stir in chickpeas, diced tomatoes, vegetable broth, carrots, zucchini, Moroccan spice blend, salt, and pepper.
4. Bring to a boil, then reduce heat and simmer for 30-40 minutes. Serve warm.

Creamy Potato and Leek Stew

Ingredients:

- 2 tablespoons butter
- 2 leeks, sliced
- 2 cups potatoes, cubed
- 4 cups vegetable broth
- 1 cup heavy cream
- Salt and pepper to taste

Instructions:

1. In a large pot, melt butter over medium heat.
2. Add leeks and sauté until softened.
3. Stir in potatoes and vegetable broth.
4. Bring to a boil, then reduce heat and simmer until potatoes are tender, about 20 minutes.
5. Stir in heavy cream, salt, and pepper, and heat through before serving.

Spicy Sausage and Kale Stew

Ingredients:

- 1 lb spicy sausage, sliced
- 2 tablespoons olive oil
- 1 onion, chopped
- 3 cloves garlic, minced
- 4 cups chicken broth
- 2 cups kale, chopped
- 2 potatoes, cubed
- 1 teaspoon red pepper flakes (optional)
- Salt and pepper to taste

Instructions:

1. In a large pot, heat olive oil over medium heat.
2. Add sausage and cook until browned.
3. Add onion and garlic, and sauté until softened.
4. Stir in chicken broth, kale, potatoes, red pepper flakes, salt, and pepper.
5. Bring to a boil, then reduce heat and simmer for 20-30 minutes. Serve warm.

Buffalo Chicken Chili

Ingredients:

- 1 lb shredded cooked chicken
- 1 can (15 oz) diced tomatoes
- 1 can (15 oz) kidney beans, rinsed and drained
- 1 onion, chopped
- 2 cloves garlic, minced
- 1/2 cup buffalo sauce
- 2 cups chicken broth
- 1 teaspoon cumin
- Salt and pepper to taste

Instructions:

1. In a large pot, sauté onion and garlic until softened.
2. Add shredded chicken, diced tomatoes, kidney beans, buffalo sauce, chicken broth, cumin, salt, and pepper.
3. Bring to a boil, then reduce heat and simmer for 20-30 minutes. Serve hot.

Enjoy your delicious stews and chilis!

Coconut Curry Lentil Stew

Ingredients:

- 1 tablespoon coconut oil
- 1 onion, chopped
- 2 cloves garlic, minced
- 1 tablespoon ginger, minced
- 1 cup lentils, rinsed
- 1 can (14 oz) coconut milk
- 4 cups vegetable broth
- 2 tablespoons curry powder
- 1 cup carrots, diced
- 1 cup spinach, chopped
- Salt and pepper to taste

Instructions:

1. In a large pot, heat coconut oil over medium heat.
2. Add onion, garlic, and ginger, and sauté until softened.
3. Stir in lentils, coconut milk, vegetable broth, curry powder, and carrots.
4. Bring to a boil, then reduce heat and simmer for 25-30 minutes until lentils are tender.
5. Stir in spinach, season with salt and pepper, and serve warm.

Tomato and Basil Stew

Ingredients:

- 2 tablespoons olive oil
- 1 onion, chopped
- 3 cloves garlic, minced
- 4 cups diced tomatoes (fresh or canned)
- 1 cup vegetable broth
- 1 teaspoon dried basil (or 1 tablespoon fresh)
- Salt and pepper to taste
- Fresh basil for garnish

Instructions:

1. In a large pot, heat olive oil over medium heat.
2. Add onion and garlic, and sauté until softened.
3. Stir in diced tomatoes, vegetable broth, dried basil, salt, and pepper.
4. Bring to a simmer and cook for 20 minutes.
5. Garnish with fresh basil before serving.

Ratatouille Stew

Ingredients:

- 2 tablespoons olive oil
- 1 onion, chopped
- 1 bell pepper, diced
- 2 zucchini, diced
- 1 eggplant, diced
- 3 cloves garlic, minced
- 4 cups diced tomatoes (fresh or canned)
- 1 teaspoon thyme
- Salt and pepper to taste

Instructions:

1. In a large pot, heat olive oil over medium heat.
2. Add onion and bell pepper, and sauté until softened.
3. Stir in zucchini, eggplant, and garlic, and cook for another 5 minutes.
4. Add diced tomatoes, thyme, salt, and pepper.
5. Simmer for 30-40 minutes until vegetables are tender. Serve warm.

Coconut Lime Chicken Stew

Ingredients:

- 1 tablespoon coconut oil
- 1 lb chicken breast, diced
- 1 onion, chopped
- 2 cloves garlic, minced
- 1 can (14 oz) coconut milk
- 1 cup chicken broth
- Zest and juice of 1 lime
- 1 cup bell peppers, diced
- 1 tablespoon ginger, minced
- Salt and pepper to taste

Instructions:

1. In a large pot, heat coconut oil over medium heat.
2. Add chicken and brown on all sides.
3. Add onion, garlic, bell peppers, and ginger, and sauté until softened.
4. Stir in coconut milk, chicken broth, lime zest, juice, salt, and pepper.
5. Bring to a simmer and cook for 20-25 minutes. Serve warm.

Classic Beef Stew

Ingredients:

- 2 lbs beef stew meat, cut into cubes
- 2 tablespoons olive oil
- 1 onion, chopped
- 4 cups beef broth
- 2 carrots, diced
- 2 potatoes, cubed
- 1 teaspoon thyme
- Salt and pepper to taste

Instructions:

1. In a large pot, heat olive oil over medium-high heat.
2. Add beef and brown on all sides.
3. Add onion and sauté until softened.
4. Stir in beef broth, carrots, potatoes, thyme, salt, and pepper.
5. Bring to a boil, then reduce heat and simmer for 1.5 to 2 hours. Serve warm.

Italian Sausage and Peppers Chili

Ingredients:

- 1 lb Italian sausage, sliced
- 1 onion, chopped
- 2 bell peppers, diced
- 2 cloves garlic, minced
- 1 can (15 oz) diced tomatoes
- 1 can (15 oz) kidney beans, rinsed and drained
- 2 tablespoons chili powder
- Salt and pepper to taste

Instructions:

1. In a large pot, brown the sausage over medium heat.
2. Add onion, bell peppers, and garlic, and sauté until softened.
3. Stir in diced tomatoes, kidney beans, chili powder, salt, and pepper.
4. Simmer for 20-30 minutes. Serve hot.

Chili con Carne

Ingredients:

- 1 lb ground beef
- 1 onion, chopped
- 2 cloves garlic, minced
- 1 can (15 oz) kidney beans, rinsed and drained
- 1 can (15 oz) diced tomatoes
- 2 tablespoons chili powder
- 1 teaspoon cumin
- Salt and pepper to taste

Instructions:

1. In a large pot, brown the ground beef over medium heat.
2. Add onion and garlic, and sauté until softened.
3. Stir in kidney beans, diced tomatoes, chili powder, cumin, salt, and pepper.
4. Simmer for 20-30 minutes. Serve hot.

Jambalaya Stew

Ingredients:

- 1 tablespoon olive oil
- 1 lb andouille sausage, sliced
- 1 lb chicken breast, diced
- 1 onion, chopped
- 1 bell pepper, diced
- 2 cloves garlic, minced
- 1 can (15 oz) diced tomatoes
- 1 cup rice
- 4 cups chicken broth
- 2 teaspoons Cajun seasoning
- Salt and pepper to taste

Instructions:

1. In a large pot, heat olive oil over medium heat.
2. Add sausage and chicken, and cook until browned.
3. Add onion, bell pepper, and garlic, and sauté until softened.
4. Stir in diced tomatoes, rice, chicken broth, Cajun seasoning, salt, and pepper.
5. Bring to a boil, then reduce heat and simmer for 20-25 minutes until rice is cooked. Serve warm.

Enjoy these hearty stews and chilis!

Smoky BBQ Bean Stew

Ingredients:

- 2 tablespoons olive oil
- 1 onion, chopped
- 2 cloves garlic, minced
- 1 bell pepper, diced
- 1 can (15 oz) black beans, rinsed and drained
- 1 can (15 oz) kidney beans, rinsed and drained
- 1 can (15 oz) diced tomatoes
- 1 cup BBQ sauce
- 1 teaspoon smoked paprika
- Salt and pepper to taste

Instructions:

1. In a large pot, heat olive oil over medium heat.
2. Add onion, garlic, and bell pepper, and sauté until softened.
3. Stir in black beans, kidney beans, diced tomatoes, BBQ sauce, smoked paprika, salt, and pepper.
4. Simmer for 20-30 minutes. Serve warm.

Turkey and Sweet Potato Chili

Ingredients:

- 1 lb ground turkey
- 1 tablespoon olive oil
- 1 onion, chopped
- 2 cloves garlic, minced
- 1 can (15 oz) diced tomatoes
- 1 cup sweet potatoes, diced
- 1 can (15 oz) black beans, rinsed and drained
- 2 tablespoons chili powder
- 1 teaspoon cumin
- Salt and pepper to taste

Instructions:

1. In a large pot, heat olive oil over medium heat.
2. Add ground turkey and brown.
3. Add onion and garlic, and sauté until softened.
4. Stir in diced tomatoes, sweet potatoes, black beans, chili powder, cumin, salt, and pepper.
5. Simmer for 30-40 minutes until sweet potatoes are tender. Serve hot.

Mediterranean Vegetable Stew

Ingredients:

- 2 tablespoons olive oil
- 1 onion, chopped
- 2 cloves garlic, minced
- 1 zucchini, diced
- 1 eggplant, diced
- 1 bell pepper, diced
- 1 can (15 oz) chickpeas, rinsed and drained
- 4 cups diced tomatoes (fresh or canned)
- 1 teaspoon oregano
- Salt and pepper to taste

Instructions:

1. In a large pot, heat olive oil over medium heat.
2. Add onion and garlic, and sauté until softened.
3. Stir in zucchini, eggplant, and bell pepper, and cook for 5-7 minutes.
4. Add chickpeas, diced tomatoes, oregano, salt, and pepper.
5. Simmer for 30 minutes. Serve warm.

Mushroom and Barley Stew

Ingredients:

- 2 tablespoons olive oil
- 1 onion, chopped
- 2 cloves garlic, minced
- 8 oz mushrooms, sliced
- 1 cup barley, rinsed
- 4 cups vegetable broth
- 2 carrots, diced
- 1 teaspoon thyme
- Salt and pepper to taste

Instructions:

1. In a large pot, heat olive oil over medium heat.
2. Add onion and garlic, and sauté until softened.
3. Stir in mushrooms and cook until they release moisture.
4. Add barley, vegetable broth, carrots, thyme, salt, and pepper.
5. Bring to a boil, then reduce heat and simmer for 40-50 minutes until barley is tender. Serve warm.

Beer-Braised Beef Stew

Ingredients:

- 2 lbs beef stew meat, cut into cubes
- 2 tablespoons olive oil
- 1 onion, chopped
- 2 cloves garlic, minced
- 1 cup beer (lager or ale)
- 4 cups beef broth
- 2 carrots, diced
- 2 potatoes, cubed
- 1 teaspoon thyme
- Salt and pepper to taste

Instructions:

1. In a large pot, heat olive oil over medium-high heat.
2. Add beef and brown on all sides.
3. Add onion and garlic, and sauté until softened.
4. Pour in beer, scraping up any browned bits.
5. Stir in beef broth, carrots, potatoes, thyme, salt, and pepper.
6. Bring to a boil, then reduce heat and simmer for 1.5 to 2 hours. Serve warm.

Indian-Spiced Lentil Chili

Ingredients:

- 2 tablespoons coconut oil
- 1 onion, chopped
- 2 cloves garlic, minced
- 1 tablespoon ginger, minced
- 1 cup lentils, rinsed
- 1 can (15 oz) diced tomatoes
- 4 cups vegetable broth
- 1 tablespoon curry powder
- 1 teaspoon cumin
- Salt and pepper to taste

Instructions:

1. In a large pot, heat coconut oil over medium heat.
2. Add onion, garlic, and ginger, and sauté until softened.
3. Stir in lentils, diced tomatoes, vegetable broth, curry powder, cumin, salt, and pepper.
4. Bring to a boil, then reduce heat and simmer for 30-40 minutes until lentils are tender. Serve hot.

Curried Butternut Squash Stew

Ingredients:

- 2 tablespoons olive oil
- 1 onion, chopped
- 2 cloves garlic, minced
- 4 cups butternut squash, cubed
- 1 can (15 oz) coconut milk
- 4 cups vegetable broth
- 1 tablespoon curry powder
- Salt and pepper to taste

Instructions:

1. In a large pot, heat olive oil over medium heat.
2. Add onion and garlic, and sauté until softened.
3. Stir in butternut squash, coconut milk, vegetable broth, curry powder, salt, and pepper.
4. Bring to a boil, then reduce heat and simmer for 25-30 minutes until squash is tender. Serve warm.

Chicken and Rice Stew

Ingredients:

- 1 tablespoon olive oil
- 1 lb chicken breast, diced
- 1 onion, chopped
- 2 cloves garlic, minced
- 4 cups chicken broth
- 1 cup rice
- 2 carrots, diced
- 1 cup peas (fresh or frozen)
- Salt and pepper to taste

Instructions:

1. In a large pot, heat olive oil over medium heat.
2. Add chicken and brown on all sides.
3. Add onion and garlic, and sauté until softened.
4. Stir in chicken broth, rice, carrots, peas, salt, and pepper.
5. Bring to a boil, then reduce heat and simmer for 20-25 minutes until rice is cooked. Serve warm.

Enjoy these hearty and flavorful stews and chilis!

Chili Verde

Ingredients:

- 1 lb pork shoulder, diced
- 2 tablespoons olive oil
- 1 onion, chopped
- 4 cloves garlic, minced
- 2 cups tomatillos, diced (or canned tomatillos)
- 1-2 jalapeños, chopped (to taste)
- 1 cup chicken broth
- 1 teaspoon cumin
- Salt and pepper to taste
- Fresh cilantro for garnish

Instructions:

1. In a large pot, heat olive oil over medium heat.
2. Add pork and brown on all sides.
3. Stir in onion and garlic, and sauté until softened.
4. Add tomatillos, jalapeños, chicken broth, cumin, salt, and pepper.
5. Simmer for 1.5 to 2 hours until pork is tender. Garnish with cilantro before serving.

Eggplant and Chickpea Stew

Ingredients:

- 2 tablespoons olive oil
- 1 onion, chopped
- 2 cloves garlic, minced
- 1 eggplant, diced
- 1 can (15 oz) chickpeas, rinsed and drained
- 1 can (15 oz) diced tomatoes
- 1 teaspoon cumin
- 1 teaspoon paprika
- Salt and pepper to taste
- Fresh parsley for garnish

Instructions:

1. In a large pot, heat olive oil over medium heat.
2. Add onion and garlic, and sauté until softened.
3. Stir in eggplant and cook for about 5 minutes.
4. Add chickpeas, diced tomatoes, cumin, paprika, salt, and pepper.
5. Simmer for 30 minutes until eggplant is tender. Garnish with parsley before serving.

Beef and Ale Stew

Ingredients:

- 2 lbs beef stew meat, cut into cubes
- 2 tablespoons olive oil
- 1 onion, chopped
- 4 cloves garlic, minced
- 1 cup ale (or stout)
- 4 cups beef broth
- 2 carrots, diced
- 2 potatoes, cubed
- 1 teaspoon thyme
- Salt and pepper to taste

Instructions:

1. In a large pot, heat olive oil over medium-high heat.
2. Add beef and brown on all sides.
3. Add onion and garlic, and sauté until softened.
4. Pour in ale, scraping up any browned bits.
5. Stir in beef broth, carrots, potatoes, thyme, salt, and pepper.
6. Bring to a boil, then reduce heat and simmer for 1.5 to 2 hours. Serve warm.

Moroccan Lamb Stew

Ingredients:

- 2 lbs lamb shoulder, cut into chunks
- 2 tablespoons olive oil
- 1 onion, chopped
- 2 cloves garlic, minced
- 1 can (15 oz) chickpeas, rinsed and drained
- 1 can (15 oz) diced tomatoes
- 2 cups vegetable broth
- 2 teaspoons cumin
- 1 teaspoon cinnamon
- Salt and pepper to taste
- Fresh cilantro for garnish

Instructions:

1. In a large pot, heat olive oil over medium heat.
2. Add lamb and brown on all sides.
3. Stir in onion and garlic, and sauté until softened.
4. Add chickpeas, diced tomatoes, vegetable broth, cumin, cinnamon, salt, and pepper.
5. Simmer for 1.5 to 2 hours until lamb is tender. Garnish with cilantro before serving.

Rustic Potato and Bacon Stew

Ingredients:

- 4 slices bacon, chopped
- 1 onion, chopped
- 2 cloves garlic, minced
- 4 cups potatoes, diced
- 4 cups chicken broth
- 1 cup heavy cream
- Salt and pepper to taste
- Fresh chives for garnish

Instructions:

1. In a large pot, cook bacon over medium heat until crispy.
2. Remove bacon and set aside, leaving fat in the pot.
3. Add onion and garlic, and sauté until softened.
4. Stir in potatoes and chicken broth, and bring to a boil.
5. Reduce heat and simmer for 20-25 minutes until potatoes are tender.
6. Stir in heavy cream, bacon, salt, and pepper. Garnish with chives before serving.

Spicy Thai Coconut Chili

Ingredients:

- 1 lb ground turkey or chicken
- 1 tablespoon coconut oil
- 1 onion, chopped
- 2 cloves garlic, minced
- 1 tablespoon ginger, minced
- 1 can (14 oz) coconut milk
- 1 can (15 oz) diced tomatoes
- 1 can (15 oz) kidney beans, rinsed and drained
- 2 tablespoons red curry paste
- Salt and pepper to taste
- Fresh cilantro for garnish

Instructions:

1. In a large pot, heat coconut oil over medium heat.
2. Add ground turkey and brown.
3. Add onion, garlic, and ginger, and sauté until softened.
4. Stir in coconut milk, diced tomatoes, kidney beans, red curry paste, salt, and pepper.
5. Simmer for 20-30 minutes. Garnish with cilantro before serving.

Cajun Chicken and Sausage Stew

Ingredients:

- 1 lb chicken thighs, diced
- 1 lb smoked sausage, sliced
- 2 tablespoons olive oil
- 1 onion, chopped
- 1 bell pepper, diced
- 2 celery stalks, diced
- 2 cloves garlic, minced
- 4 cups chicken broth
- 2 cups diced tomatoes
- 2 tablespoons Cajun seasoning
- Salt and pepper to taste

Instructions:

1. In a large pot, heat olive oil over medium heat.
2. Add chicken and sausage, and brown.
3. Add onion, bell pepper, celery, and garlic, and sauté until softened.
4. Stir in chicken broth, diced tomatoes, Cajun seasoning, salt, and pepper.
5. Simmer for 30-40 minutes. Serve warm.

Beef and Vegetable Chili

Ingredients:

- 1 lb ground beef
- 1 tablespoon olive oil
- 1 onion, chopped
- 2 cloves garlic, minced
- 1 bell pepper, diced
- 1 can (15 oz) kidney beans, rinsed and drained
- 1 can (15 oz) diced tomatoes
- 2 tablespoons chili powder
- 1 teaspoon cumin
- Salt and pepper to taste

Instructions:

1. In a large pot, heat olive oil over medium heat.
2. Add ground beef and brown.
3. Add onion, garlic, and bell pepper, and sauté until softened.
4. Stir in kidney beans, diced tomatoes, chili powder, cumin, salt, and pepper.
5. Simmer for 20-30 minutes. Serve hot.

Enjoy these delicious stews and chilis!

Thai Green Curry Stew

Ingredients:

- 1 lb chicken breast, diced
- 1 tablespoon coconut oil
- 1 onion, chopped
- 2 cloves garlic, minced
- 1 tablespoon ginger, minced
- 2-3 tablespoons green curry paste (to taste)
- 1 can (14 oz) coconut milk
- 1 cup vegetable or chicken broth
- 2 cups mixed vegetables (bell pepper, zucchini, etc.)
- Fresh basil for garnish
- Lime wedges for serving

Instructions:

1. In a large pot, heat coconut oil over medium heat.
2. Add chicken and cook until browned.
3. Stir in onion, garlic, and ginger, and sauté until softened.
4. Add green curry paste and stir for a minute.
5. Pour in coconut milk and broth, then add mixed vegetables.
6. Simmer for 20-25 minutes until chicken is cooked through and vegetables are tender. Garnish with fresh basil and serve with lime wedges.

Rustic Italian Bean Stew

Ingredients:

- 2 tablespoons olive oil
- 1 onion, chopped
- 2 cloves garlic, minced
- 1 carrot, diced
- 1 celery stalk, diced
- 2 cans (15 oz each) mixed beans, rinsed and drained
- 1 can (15 oz) diced tomatoes
- 4 cups vegetable broth
- 1 teaspoon Italian seasoning
- Salt and pepper to taste
- Fresh parsley for garnish

Instructions:

1. In a large pot, heat olive oil over medium heat.
2. Add onion, garlic, carrot, and celery, and sauté until softened.
3. Stir in mixed beans, diced tomatoes, vegetable broth, Italian seasoning, salt, and pepper.
4. Simmer for 30 minutes. Garnish with fresh parsley before serving.

Sweet Corn and Chicken Chili

Ingredients:

- 1 lb chicken breast, diced
- 2 tablespoons olive oil
- 1 onion, chopped
- 2 cloves garlic, minced
- 2 cans (15 oz each) sweet corn, drained
- 1 can (15 oz) diced tomatoes
- 1 can (15 oz) black beans, rinsed and drained
- 1 tablespoon chili powder
- 1 teaspoon cumin
- Salt and pepper to taste

Instructions:

1. In a large pot, heat olive oil over medium heat.
2. Add chicken and brown.
3. Stir in onion and garlic, and sauté until softened.
4. Add sweet corn, diced tomatoes, black beans, chili powder, cumin, salt, and pepper.
5. Simmer for 20-30 minutes. Serve warm.

Lamb and White Bean Stew

Ingredients:

- 2 lbs lamb shoulder, cut into chunks
- 2 tablespoons olive oil
- 1 onion, chopped
- 2 cloves garlic, minced
- 1 can (15 oz) white beans, rinsed and drained
- 4 cups chicken or vegetable broth
- 2 carrots, diced
- 1 teaspoon rosemary
- Salt and pepper to taste

Instructions:

1. In a large pot, heat olive oil over medium heat.
2. Add lamb and brown on all sides.
3. Stir in onion and garlic, and sauté until softened.
4. Add white beans, broth, carrots, rosemary, salt, and pepper.
5. Simmer for 1.5 to 2 hours until lamb is tender. Serve warm.

Thai Red Curry Beef Stew

Ingredients:

- 1 lb beef stew meat, cut into cubes
- 1 tablespoon coconut oil
- 1 onion, chopped
- 2 cloves garlic, minced
- 2-3 tablespoons red curry paste (to taste)
- 1 can (14 oz) coconut milk
- 2 cups beef broth
- 2 cups mixed vegetables (bell pepper, broccoli, etc.)
- Fresh cilantro for garnish

Instructions:

1. In a large pot, heat coconut oil over medium heat.
2. Add beef and brown on all sides.
3. Stir in onion and garlic, and sauté until softened.
4. Add red curry paste and stir for a minute.
5. Pour in coconut milk and beef broth, then add mixed vegetables.
6. Simmer for 1-1.5 hours until beef is tender. Garnish with fresh cilantro before serving.

Classic Split Pea Soup

Ingredients:

- 1 lb split peas, rinsed
- 2 tablespoons olive oil
- 1 onion, chopped
- 2 carrots, diced
- 2 celery stalks, diced
- 4 cloves garlic, minced
- 6 cups vegetable or chicken broth
- 1 bay leaf
- Salt and pepper to taste
- Fresh parsley for garnish

Instructions:

1. In a large pot, heat olive oil over medium heat.
2. Add onion, carrots, celery, and garlic, and sauté until softened.
3. Stir in split peas, broth, bay leaf, salt, and pepper.
4. Bring to a boil, then reduce heat and simmer for 1-1.5 hours until peas are soft.
5. Remove bay leaf, blend if desired for a creamy texture, and garnish with fresh parsley before serving.

Enjoy these hearty and flavorful stews and soups!

Black Eyed Pea and Collard Green Stew

Ingredients:

- 1 tablespoon olive oil
- 1 onion, chopped
- 2 cloves garlic, minced
- 4 cups collard greens, chopped
- 2 cans (15 oz each) black-eyed peas, rinsed and drained
- 4 cups vegetable broth
- 1 teaspoon thyme
- 1 teaspoon smoked paprika
- Salt and pepper to taste
- Hot sauce (optional)

Instructions:

1. In a large pot, heat olive oil over medium heat.
2. Add onion and garlic, and sauté until softened.
3. Stir in collard greens and cook until wilted.
4. Add black-eyed peas, vegetable broth, thyme, smoked paprika, salt, and pepper.
5. Simmer for 20-30 minutes. Serve hot, with hot sauce if desired.

Tomato Basil Chickpea Stew

Ingredients:

- 1 tablespoon olive oil
- 1 onion, chopped
- 2 cloves garlic, minced
- 2 cans (15 oz each) chickpeas, rinsed and drained
- 1 can (28 oz) crushed tomatoes
- 2 cups vegetable broth
- 1 teaspoon dried basil
- 1 teaspoon oregano
- Salt and pepper to taste
- Fresh basil for garnish

Instructions:

1. In a large pot, heat olive oil over medium heat.
2. Add onion and garlic, and sauté until softened.
3. Stir in chickpeas, crushed tomatoes, vegetable broth, dried basil, oregano, salt, and pepper.
4. Simmer for 20-30 minutes. Garnish with fresh basil before serving.

Spicy Pumpkin and Black Bean Chili

Ingredients:

- 1 tablespoon olive oil
- 1 onion, chopped
- 2 cloves garlic, minced
- 1 can (15 oz) black beans, rinsed and drained
- 1 can (15 oz) pumpkin puree
- 1 can (14 oz) diced tomatoes
- 2 cups vegetable broth
- 2 tablespoons chili powder
- 1 teaspoon cumin
- 1-2 jalapeños, chopped (to taste)
- Salt and pepper to taste

Instructions:

1. In a large pot, heat olive oil over medium heat.
2. Add onion and garlic, and sauté until softened.
3. Stir in black beans, pumpkin puree, diced tomatoes, vegetable broth, chili powder, cumin, jalapeños, salt, and pepper.
4. Simmer for 30 minutes. Serve warm.

Fish and Vegetable Stew

Ingredients:

- 1 tablespoon olive oil
- 1 onion, chopped
- 2 cloves garlic, minced
- 1 bell pepper, diced
- 2 carrots, sliced
- 2 zucchinis, diced
- 4 cups fish stock (or vegetable broth)
- 1 lb white fish (like cod or tilapia), cut into chunks
- 1 can (14 oz) diced tomatoes
- 1 teaspoon thyme
- Salt and pepper to taste
- Fresh parsley for garnish

Instructions:

1. In a large pot, heat olive oil over medium heat.
2. Add onion and garlic, and sauté until softened.
3. Stir in bell pepper, carrots, and zucchini, and cook for about 5 minutes.
4. Pour in fish stock, add diced tomatoes, thyme, salt, and pepper. Bring to a boil.
5. Reduce heat and add fish, simmering for about 10 minutes until cooked through. Garnish with fresh parsley before serving.

Enjoy these wholesome and delicious stews!

www.ingramcontent.com/pod-product-compliance
Lightning Source LLC
LaVergne TN
LVHW081333060526
838201LV00055B/2612